All the Phi-nest Recipes

A Collection of Recipes From the Sisters of Phi Mu Phi Gamma

Published by Duncurra LLC

DEDICATION

This cookbook is dedicated to Wendy Bowman Bishop, the Phi Mu Phi Gamma Chapter Adviser, Spring 2012 to Fall 2015. Thank you for all of your support and guidance.

FORWARD

Phi Mu Fraternity for Women was founded in 1852 at Wesleyan College in Macon, Georgia. Phi Mu is a women's organization which provides personal and academic development, service to others, commitment to excellence and lifelong friendship through a shared tradition. The Phi Mu Foundation is an organization committed to "the development of women" through leadership and scholarship programs, as well assistance to members in times of need.

Phi Mu Foundation funds values-based leadership programs for current and emerging leaders. One such program is the Undergraduate Interfraternity Institute (UIFI), which is a leadership experience held every two years, and it offers Phi Mu members the opportunity to explore, define, and enhance leadership skills to take to their chapter. Phi Mu Foundation also offers scholarships that financially assist with academic and life goals. There are scholarships based on both merit and financial need.

The Foundation also gives assistance to members and their families during times of need, such as natural disasters, medical emergencies, and other serious personal issues. The financial assistance given goes towards purchasing food, clothing, housing, books and school supplies, medical care, and other necessities.

Phi Mu Foundation states their mission is "The lifetime development of women through the support of Phi Mu's leadership, scholarship, philanthropic and educational programs, and historic preservation."

The sisters of the Phi Gamma chapter of Phi Mu have directly benefited from leadership and scholarship programs, and have experienced the true meaning of The Foundation's goal of "Sisters Helping Sisters."

Therefore, the sisters of the Phi Gamma chapter of Phi Mu will donate all proceeds from the sale of this cookbook to the Phi Mu Foundation.

TABLE OF CONTENTS

ഔ BEVERAGES ଔ

Indian Chai

Contributed by Avanti Mehta

Ingredients (Serves 6)

¼ cup milk

6 cups water

½ teaspoon fresh grated ginger, or ¼ teaspoon powdered ginger

12 teaspoon sugar

Fresh mint

6 teaspoon black tea (may empty contents of 6 tea bags)

1 teaspoon freshly ground cardamom, or ½ teaspoon cardamom powder

Instructions

Place the water in a deep pan and cook on medium-high heat. As the water begins to heat up, add the black tea and fresh ginger. When water starts to boil, add the milk and turn the heat to medium. As it begins to boil again, add the sugar and mint, and reduce the heat to low. Simmer for 10 to 15 minutes on low heat. Remove from heat, and serve.

Cafe Sua Da (Vietnamese Iced Coffee)

Contributed by Julie Doan

Ingredients
Medium coarse ground coffee
Sweetened condensed milk
1 empty glass
1 glass filled with ice
Vietnamese coffee press

Instructions
Add 3 tablespoons (or however according to your preference in sweetness) of the sweetened condensed milk to the empty glass. Add 3 tablespoons of the ground coffee into the coffee press. Pack it well, and screw the press on. Pour boiling water into the press, and wait for the coffee to drip into the cup with the condensed milk. Once done, stir the coffee and condensed milk together. Pour over the glass of ice.

Dorm Friendly Version
Make any sort of black coffee normally, and mix it with sweetened condensed milk. Add ice.

Iced Tea

Contributed by Olivia Conn

Ingredients
4 Celestial Seasoning Tea Bags (Lemon
    Zinger)
4 Celestial Seasoning Tea Bags (Red Zinger)
4 cups pure apple juice
4 cups water

Instructions
Steep tea bags in boiling water for 10 minutes.
Combine with juice and refrigerate until cold.

Dorm Friendly Iced Coffee

Contributed by Sayre Posey

Ingredients
1/2 cup of coffee
1/2 cup of milk
2 tablespoons sugar
Ice

Instructions
Fill a tall glass halfway with ice. Pour in
enough coffee to reach the ice line, and then
fill the rest of the glass with milk. Add a
spoonful of sugar and serve.

Easy Punch

Contributed by Meghan Cusack

Ingredients
2 quarts raspberry Kool-Aid prepared
1 small can frozen lemonade
1 small can frozen orange juice
2 quarts ginger ale, chilled

Instructions
Combine first 3 ingredients, chill. When ready
serve pour juice and Kool-Aid mixture in a
punch bowl and gently add ginger ale.

Easier Punch

Contributed by Meghan Cusack

Ingredients
1 pint any flavor sherbet
2 quarts ginger ale, chilled

Instructions
Place sherbet in a punch bowl. Gently pour
chilled ginger ale over sherbet. You can also
serve in tall glasses instead of as a punch. Put
2 scoops sherbet in glass, fill with ginger ale.

17

Peanut Butter and Banana Protein Smoothie

Contributed by Kyarii Ramarui

Ingredients
1 cup of milk
1 frozen banana
2½ tablespoons of peanut butter, almond butter, or Nutella
1 scoop of vanilla whey protein powder
1 teaspoon of chia seeds
¾ cup of ice
⅛ teaspoon of cinnamon

Instructions
Place banana, ice, peanut/almond butter, and milk into a blender and pulse until all the ingredients are incorporated. Add remaining ingredients and blend until fully mixed.

Morning Smoothie

Contributed by Bethale Kindane

Ingredients
Mixed berries
Orange juice
Water
Seeds of your choice (flax, chia, almonds)

Instructions
Place seeds in bottom of blender. Add in the berries. Pour in a desired amount of orange juice. Add enough water to cover all the ingredients. For a thicker smoothie, use less water, but still enough to cover 75% of ingredients. Grind first to pulverize the seeds, then puree and liquefy the mixture until you reach a desired consistency.

Protein Energy Smoothie

Contributed by Bethale Kidane

Ingredients
Almonds
1 whole peach
4 strawberries cut into fourths
2 cups of blueberries
Spinach
Soy milk
Water

Instructions
Place almonds bottom of blender. Add in half of fruit. Add desired amount of spinach. Add remaining fruit. Add soy milk to cover 25-50% of the ingredients. Add water to cover ingredients. Grind the mix until the almonds are pulverized, then puree, and liquefy the mixture until you reach a desired consistency.

Berry Smoothie

Contributed by Jessica Deng

Ingredients
4 large frozen strawberries
⅓ cup frozen berries
¼ cup of greek yogurt
1 tablespoon honey
1 cup orange juice

Instructions
Combine in blender to an even consistency.

Mixed Fruit Smoothie

Contributed by Muskan Pathak

Ingredients
1 cup of almond milk
Ice (optional)
Handful of spinach
¼ cup of strawberries
¼ cup of blueberries
¼ cup of raspberries
¼ cup of blackberries
1 banana
Chia seeds (optional)
1 teaspoon of honey

Instructions
Combine in blender to an even consistency.

Friendship Tea

Contributed by Author, Ceci Giltenan

Ingredients

1 cup instant tea
1 ½ cup sugar
2 cup Tang instant breakfast drink
1 cup dried lemonade mix
2 tsp cinnamon
2 tsp cloves

Instructions

Mix all ingredients thoroughly. Store in airtight container. To serve add 1 teaspoon to 1 cup hot water. Use more or less to taste.

Hot Spiced Punch

Contributed by Author, Ceci Giltenan

Ingredients

2 ¼ C pineapple juice
1 ¾ C water
2 C cranberry juice
½ C brown sugar
1 tablespoon each whole cloves, whole allspice and broken cinnamon sticks

Instructions

Mix first 4 ingredients in saucepan, heat. Put spices in tea infuser. Steep in simmering liquid. Serve warm.

❧ SOUPS ❧

Maryland Crab Soup I

Contributed by Lauren Goodwin

Ingredients
1 pound bag of mixed vegetables
1 32 ounce can of petite chopped tomatoes
1 pound lump crab claw meat
1 large box of chicken stock
1 can diced potatoes
1 pound frozen shrimp or diced beef
Optional for a heartier soup

Instructions
Pour all of the ingredients into a large pot. Stir until well mixed. Heat on the stove at medium temperature until warm, then serve.

"There is a saying in Baltimore that crabs may be prepared in fifty ways and that all of them are good."

~ H. L. Mencken

Maryland Crab Soup II

Contributed by Meghan Cusack

Ingredients
2 tablespoons olive oil
1 cup each chopped onion, celery and carrots
4 cloves garlic minced or crushed
1 quart chicken broth
2 potatoes peeled and cut into bite sized cubes
1 14.5 oz. can each green beans (with liquid)
1 14.5 oz. can corn (with liquid)
1 14.5 oz. can tomatoes
1 14.5 oz. can tomato sauce
1/4 cup Old Bay Seasoning
1 tablespoon sugar
1 quart water
1 lb crab meat

Instructions
Heat olive oil in a large stock pot and add onion, celery, carrots and garlic. Sauté until onions are soft. Add all remaining ingredients. Bring to boil and reduce heat to simmer. Allow to simmer until potatoes and carrots are tender.

Rustic Tortellini Soup

Contributed by Erin O'Sullivan

Ingredients
5 to 6 Italian turkey sausage links
1 medium onion, chopped
4 garlic cloves, minced
2 - 32 ounce reduced-sodium chicken broth
1¾ cups water
2 cans petite diced tomatoes, undrained
1 - 20 ounce package refrigerated cheese
    tortellini
1 - 9 ounce package fresh baby spinach,
    coarsely chopped
2¼ teaspoons fresh basil, minced
    (substitution: 1 teaspoon dried basil)
¼ teaspoon pepper
Crushed red pepper flakes
Shredded parmesan cheese *optional*

Instructions
Slice the sausage into quarter size rounds. In a
large pot, add the onion, and cook over
medium heat until meat is no longer pink.
Add the garlic and cook for an additional
minute. Stir in the broth, water, and tomatoes.
Bring to a boil. Add the tortellini, and return
to a boil. Cook for seven to nine minutes or
until tender, stirring occasionally. Reduce heat;

add the spinach, basil, pepper, and pepper flakes. Cook two to three minutes longer or until the spinach is wilted. Serve with cheese if desired.

Spicy Broccoli Cheese Soup

Contributed by Meghan Cusack

Ingredients
1 large onion in sautéed in 4 oz butter
1 can cream of mushroom soup,
1 can cream of celery soup
1 can cream of chicken soup
3 cans milk
1 lb Mexican Style Velveeta cubed
2 boxes frozen chopped broccoli micro waved and drained

Instructions
Heat soups and milk add cheese and broccoli and simmer until cheese is melted and the soups are blended. If you like a little more spice add chopped jalapeno peppers. If you don't like spicy food, use regular Velveeta. Excellent freshly cooked but improves with age.

Betsy's Minestrone Soup

Contributed by Valerie Stone

Ingredients

1 large leek, thinly sliced (substitution: medium yellow onion)
2 carrots, chopped
1 cup spinach, chopped (fresh or frozen)
½ cup green beans, halved (fresh is better, but canned are fine)
2 stalks celery, thinly sliced
1 teaspoon garlic powder
1 teaspoon onion powder
3 large cloves garlic, finely chopped
4 dashes hot pepper sauce (optional)
3 tablespoon olive oil
6 cups chicken stock
1 14 ounce can petite diced tomatoes
1 12 ounce can v8
1 tablespoon fresh basil, chopped (substitution: 2 teaspoon, dried)
1 teaspoon fresh thyme (substitution: 1/2 teaspoon, dried)
Salt
Ground black pepper
2 cups small pasta shapes (cooked, drained, and rinsed)
1 can cannellini or kidney beans (rinsed and drained)

Instructions

Put vegetables in a large saucepan with the olive oil. Heat until sizzling. Lower heat and cover for 15 minutes. Stir occasionally. Add stock, V8, tomatoes, herbs, and seasoning. Bring to a boil, reduce heat, replace lid and simmer gently for 30 minutes. Add beans and pasta and simmer for another 10 minutes. Check the seasoning and serve hot. Sprinkle with parmesan cheese.

Fresh Vegetable Soup

Contributed by Author Ceci Giltenan

Ingredients

¼ cup diced onion
2 cups chicken broth
2 cloves garlic minced
1 cups thinly sliced zucchini
½ C thinly sliced carrots
½ C chopped tomato
1 tsp chopped fresh parsley
¼ tsp basil leaves
⅛ tsp black pepper

Instructions

In a 1 ½ quart non-stick sauce pan combine the ingredients and cook over low heat until vegetables are Tender . Makes 2 servings.

Sweet Potato Soup

Contributed by Cecilia Grady

Ingredients
2 tablespoon vegetable oil
1 onion
1 tablespoon fresh ginger
1 tablespoon gluten free thai red curry paste
1 teaspoon salt
1 1/2 pounds sweet potatoes
1 14 ounces can light coconut milk
4 cups gluten-free vegetable stock
1 lime
1/2 cup fresh cilantro

Instructions
Prepare ingredients separately by dicing the onion, finely chopping the ginger, peeling and dicing the sweet potatoes, juicing the lime, and chopping the cilantro. Heat oil on medium-high heat in a large saucepan. Add diced onion and ginger, cook until soft (about 5 minutes), stirring often. Add salt and curry paste and stir for about 1 minute. Add sweet potatoes, coconut milk, vegetable stock, and 1/4 cup cilantro, and bring to a boil. Reduce heat to medium and simmer, uncovered, for 20 to 25 minutes, or until sweet potatoes are soft. Remove from the heat. Puree soup in

batches with a blender or food processor, or using an immersion blender. Return soup to the heat and bring back to a simmer. Stir in the lime juice, and heat for two minutes. Serve, garnished with the remaining cilantro.

Filipino Soup Sinigang

Contributed by Ashley Porter

Ingredients
1 packet of tamarind soup base
8 cups of water
2 teaspoons pepper
1 pound of meat (chicken, shrimp, fish)
1 tomato quartered
1 cup each whole okra
1 cup green beans
1 banana pepper *optional*
2 cups spinach
2 cups broccoli
3 cups rice cooked

Instructions
Boil water in a large pot. Add tamarind soup base and pepper. Add meat. Simmer for 5 minutes on medium heat (or until meat is cooked through). Increase heat to high. Add tomato, okra, green beans, banana pepper, broccoli. Boil 20 minutes. Add spinach. Boil 5 more minutes. Serve over cooked white rice.

Potato Leek Soup

Contributed by Emily Murphy

Ingredients
3 to 4 pounds white potatoes
1 leek
32 ounce chicken stock
1 to 2 tablespoons light olive oil
1 tablespoon salt
½ cup half and half or heavy cream

Instructions
Trim the leek where the stock turns light green. Cut it in half lengthwise and rinse very well in cold water. Dry well. Cut leek halves into ¼ inch sections, set aside. Peel and cut the potatoes into ½ inch cubes. Set aside. Heat olive oil in a large stockpot over medium heat. Once hot, add the leeks and stir constantly until they soften, about three to four minutes. Do not overcook. Add the chicken stock, potatoes, salt, and enough water to cover the potatoes. Cover and bring to a boil. Boil for 12 to 15 minutes, or until the potatoes are cooked through but still firm. Cool slightly. In two batches, add about a quarter of the cooked potatoes and enough stock to cover them to a blender. Blend until smooth. Return each batch to the stockpot.

Heat the stockpot over low heat until warm.
Stir in the half and half , salt, and pepper to
taste. Serve warm with bread or crackers.

*"I feed on good soup, not beautiful
language."*

~ Molière

ℬ BREADS ℭ

Dark Chocolate Chip Banana Bread with a Secret Twist!

Contributed by Yoo-Jin Kang

Ingredients:
2 avocados- ripe
2 bananas- ripe
3 tablespoons almond milk
1 teaspoon lemon juice
3 tablespoons coconut oil
2 cups whole wheat flour
3/4 cup dark brown sugar
1 teaspoon cinnamon
1 teaspoon baking powder
1 teaspoon baking soda
1 teaspoon salt
1/4 cup dark chocolate cocoa powder
Optional: 1/4 cup dark chocolate chips

Instructions:
Preheat oven to 350. Whisk dry ingredients in a bowl set aside. Mash up bananas and avocados, add the lemon juice and almond milk. Melt coconut oil in a bowl (microwave will do!) and add to wet ingredients. Add the

wet ingredients to dry and mix till just combined! You don't want to over mix! Place in 9x5 standard loaf pan and bake for about 40-50 minutes until a toothpick comes out clean!

Note: Allow the bread to cool- when it is fresh out of the oven you might still smell the avocado but once it's cool- it's just yummy fudgy goodness!

Beer Bread

Contributed by Katharine Shaver

Ingredients
3 cups self rising flour
2 tablespoons sugar
12 ounces beer

Instructions
Mix together the flour, sugar, and beer in a large bowl. Prepare a baking pan and pour in the mixture. Bake at 350◦ for 45 minutes.

Irish Brown Soda Bread

Contributed by Author Ceci Giltenan

Ingredients
1 teaspoon salt
1 teaspoon sugar
1 heaping teaspoon cream of tartar
1 heaping teaspoon baking soda
1 cups all-purpose flour
3 cups whole wheat flour
2 cups sour milk or buttermilk

Instructions
Sift salt, sugar, cream of tartar, baking soda and All-purpose flour. Add whole wheat flour and lift handfuls to aerate. Make a well in center and add liquid mixing until dough leaves sides of bowl. Knead slightly; form into a slightly flattened ball. Cut a cross in the loaf. Bake at 400 for 40 minutes. Turn loaf upside down and return to oven for 5 minutes.

For **White Soda Bread**, use 4 cups all-purpose flour and omit whole wheat flour. One 1 cup raisins can be added if desired.

Cranberry Apple Bread

Contributed by Author Ceci Giltenan

Ingredients
3 cups flour
1 cup sugar
2 teaspoons baking powder
½ teaspoon salt
½ teaspoon baking soda
2 beaten eggs
1 cup apple juice
2/3 cup milk
½ teaspoon almond extract
¼ cup vegetable oil
¾ cup chopped or slivered almonds
¾ cup coarsely chopped cranberries
¾ cup coarsely chopped apples
2 teaspoons finely shredded orange peel

Instructions
Grease the bottom of a 9x5x3 inch loaf pan. In one bowl combine all dry ingredients well. In another bowl combine all liquid ingredients, stirring well to combine. Add liquid ingredients to dry ingredients stirring to combine. Fold in fruit and nuts. Pour batter in pan and bake at 350 for 1 hour. Loaf is done when a toothpick inserted in the center comes out clean.

Zucchini Bread

Contributed by Juliana Venegas

Ingredients
1 cup oil
2 cups sugar
3 eggs
2 cups grated zucchini
2 teaspoons vanilla extract
3 cups flour
1 teaspoon salt
1 teaspoon baking soda
¼ teaspoon baking powder
3 teaspoons cinnamon

Instructions
Preheat oven to 350 degrees. Mix all ingredients in order given. Pour into two greased loaf pans. Bake for 1 hour or until a toothpick inserted in the middle comes out clean.

"All sorrows are less with bread."
~ Miguel de Cervantes, Don Quixote

ଚ SALADS ଓ

Apple-Spinach Salad

Contributed by Erin O'Sullivan

Ingredients
1 10 ounce package fresh spinach, torn
2 granny smith apples, chopped
½ cup cashews
¼ cup golden raisins
¼ cup sugar
¼ cup apple cider vinegar
¼ cup vegetable oil
¼ teaspoon garlic salt
¼ teaspoon celery salt

Instructions
Combine the spinach, apples, cashews, and raisins in a large bowl. Combine the sugar, vinegar, oil, garlic salt, and celery salt in a jar. Cover it tightly, and shake vigorously. Pour it over the spinach mixture, tossing gently.

Seven Layer Salad

Contributed by Baonhu Ky

Ingredients
1 bag Sargento 4 cheese Mexican
2 romaine lettuce hearts
4 tomatoes
1 box of rice pilaf
1 green, 1 red and 1 yellow pepper
Avocados
2 tablespoon sour cream
3 tablespoon ranch

Instructions
Wash vegetables. Dice tomatoes and peppers. Chop lettuce into bite size pieces. Cook rice pilaf according to the box's instructions.Peel the avocado and cut into thin slices. Lay a bottom layer of lettuce, about half an inch thick.Add the next layer of tomatoes. Add another thin layer of lettuce.Put the diced pieces of peppers on top of the lettuce. Add another thin layer of lettuce. Add the rice pilaf on top of the lettuce. Add another thin layer of lettuce. Lay the slices of avocado evenly on top of the lettuce.In a bowl, combine ranch, sour cream and mix. Spread the mixture on top of the avocado layer.Sprinkle the cheese on top of the mixture.

Summer Asparagus and Tomato Salad

Contributed by Emily Bordenski

Ingredients
1 pound asparagus spears
1 pint cherry tomatoes, halved
½ small red onion, diced finely
3 tablespoons capers, drained
2 cloves of garlic, minced
3 tablespoons extra virgin olive oil
1½ tablespoons red wine vinegar
1 tablespoons fresh lemon juice
Sea salt
Water
Fresh ground black pepper

Instructions
Prepare the asparagus by breaking off bottom ends and cutting the into one inch pieces. Bring three to four cups of water to boil in a medium pot, add asparagus and cook until tender (about 1 ½ minutes). Drain and add asparagus to an ice bath, briefly to stop the cooking process. Drain well, add to a large serving bowl. Add onions, tomatoes, garlic, and capers. Toss in olive oil, vinegar, and lemon juice. Season with salt and pepper. Chill 2-3 hours before serving for best results.

Quinoa Salad

Contributed by Vanessa Berruetta

Ingredients
2 cups quinoa
3 cups water
1 jalapeno
½ onion
4 garlic cloves
1 bell pepper
1 can whole kernel corn
1 can black beans
1/3 cup cilantro
3 tomatoes
Sauce:
1/3 cup olive oil
1 tablespoon salt
2 juiced limes

Instructions
Bring water to a boil, add quinoa. Reduce heat to low, and simmer for 15 minutes, or until the water is gone. Finely chop jalapeno, onion, garlic, bell pepper, and cilantro. Strain excess water from the corn and beans. Mix with chopped ingredients. Add the cooked quinoa. Blend together sauce ingredients and mix into the quinoa salad. Serve with tortilla chips or eat plainly for a healthy snack.

Easy To Make Egg-Potato Salad

Contributed by Baonhu Ky

Ingredients
6 small potatoes
12 eggs
Mayonnaise
Relish
Paprika
Pepper

Instructions
Boil the potatoes and eggs until cooked. Peel the eggs and potatoes and rinse them in water to fully clean them. Dice the eggs and potatoes into about three quarters of an inch wide. Mix in bowl with the desired amount of mayonnaise. Add a lot of mayonnaise if you want a smooth and thicker texture. Add about 2 teaspoons of relish and add pepper for taste, mix. Once mixed, sprinkle a little bit of paprika on top to give it some color.

Watermelon Cucumber Salad

Contributed by Kathleen Britt

Ingredients
3 cups chopped watermelon
1 cup chopped cucumbers
½ cup crumbled mild feta cheese
2 tablespoons chopped fresh mint
2 tablespoons balsamic vinaigrette dressing

Instructions
Combine the watermelon, cucumbers, feta cheese, mint, and dressing. Serve immediately.

"Salad can get a bad rap. People think of bland and watery iceberg lettuce, but in fact, salads are an art form, from the simplest rendition to a colorful kitchen-sink approach."
~ Marcus Samuelsson

ℬ APPETIZERS ℰ

Crispy Corn
Contributed by Sushmitha Kavuru

Ingredients
1 cup corn kernels
2-3 tablespoons all-purpose flour
½ teaspoon salt
Pepper
Garlic powder
Sweet and sour sauce

Instructions
Before beginning, heat up oil in a deep pan to do deep frying. In a bowl filled with a cup of corn kernels, add 2-3 tablespoons of all purpose flour. To the mixture, add 1/2 teaspoon of salt, a pinch of pepper, and sprinkle desired amount of garlic powder. Then add 3 tablespoons of water. You can either shake it or use your hand to mix the contents of the bowl together. Slowly deep fry the kernels in the oil until golden brown. Best served hot and crispy with sweet and sour sauce.

7 Layers of Heaven dip

Contributed by Audrey Petrauli

Ingredients
1 pound ground beef
2 teaspoon chipotle seasoning
1 cup salsa
3 avocados
1 teaspoon lime juice
1 teaspoon salt
1 teaspoon black pepper
3 cups shredded 4 cheese Mexican cheese
2 cups 4 cheese Mexican cheese blended
2 cups shredded lettuce
½ cup diced tomato
½ cup scallion for garnish

Instructions
Mix ground beef with chipotle seasoning, brown and drain the water. Scoop avocados and blend it for 5 seconds, add lime juice, salt, and black pepper to guacamole. Prepare a pan and put lettuce in the bottom. Continue to add these in order: Blended cheese, diced tomato, guacamole, salsa, ground beef, and top it off with shredded cheese. Sprinkle scallion for garnish.

Guacamole

Contributed by Jessica Deng

Ingredients
⅓ tomato
⅓ red onion
½ jalapeño pepper *optional*
1 large avocado
½ teaspoon lime juice
½ teaspoon lemon juice
5 sprigs of cilantro
Salt

Instructions
Dice up the tomato, onion, pepper, and cilantro finely. Cut the avocado in half down the long center and twist to open. Remove the pit. Peel the avocado. Slice the avocado into a bowl. With a fork, mash the avocado until the consistency is smooth. Add the tomato, onion, and pepper. Mix. Add the lime juice, lemon juice, salt, and cilantro. Mix again.

Buffalo Chicken Dip

Contributed by Lauren Goodwin

Ingredients
4 chicken breasts
3 8oz Kraft Philadelphia cream cheese
2 cups shredded Kraft sharp cheddar
16oz Marie's blue cheese dressing
16oz Texas Pete wing sauce
Blue Cheese Crumbles *optional*

Instructions
Cook the chicken breast fully. Shred the chicken breast, using a fork. Soften and combine the cream cheese, dressing, cheddar cheese, and chicken. Stir until well mixed. Add the hot sauce to taste. Place the mixture into a baking dish and heat at 350 degrees until warm. Serve with bread slices or tortilla chips.

Sausage Balls

Contributed by Meghan Cusack

Ingredients:
1 lb lean hot pork sausage,
½ lb sharp cheddar cheese
3 C Bisquick baking mix

Instructions:
Preheat oven to 350º. Mix together sausage, cheese and Bisquick. Roll into ¾" balls. Place balls on cookie sheet about 1"inch apart.
Bake for 15 min.

Six Minute Maryland Crab Dip

Contributed by Lauren Goodwin

Ingredients
1 pound Lump Crab Claw Meat
3 8oz packages of cream cheese
Old Bay Seasoning

Instructions
Soften and mix the cream cheese and crab meat together until well blended. Add the Old Bay seasoning to taste. Heat the mix at 350 degrees until the top is browned or until warm. Serve with crackers, bread slices, or tortilla chips.

Hot Artichoke Dip

Contributed by Olivia Conn

Ingredients
2 Cans Of Artichoke Hearts
1 Package Cream Cheese
1 Small Onion
½ Cup Mayonnaise
3-4 Cloves Garlic
1 Cup Parmesan

Instructions
Place garlic, onion, in a food processor. Pulse multiple times. Add the artichokes and pulse some more. Then add cream cheese, mayonnaise, and parmesan cheese. Bake at 350 degrees for 20-25 minutes.

Red Potato Chips

Contributed by Anlara McKenzie

Ingredients
Small red potatoes
Olive oil
Salt
Pepper
Garlic Powder
Parsley
Thyme

48

Instructions
Slice small red potatoes about 1/8th to 1/4th of an inch thick. Coat slices in olive oil, and sprinkle with salt, pepper, garlic powder, parsley and thyme. Place slices flat on tin foil covered cookie sheet. Bake in oven at 350 degrees until desired crispiness.

Crab Dip
Contributed by Nicole Magin

Ingredients
1 8 ounce package cream cheese
1 tablespoon milk
16 ounce can of crab meat
2 teaspoon Worcestershire sauce
2 tablespoon chopped onion
Shredded cheese *optional*

Instructions
Combine cheese, milk, and Worcestershire sauce. Add the onion and crab meat. Place the mixture in a small buttered dish and bake for 15 minutes at 350 degrees. If desired, sprinkle the cheese on top and melt in the oven for a few minutes. Serve with crackers.

Dorm Friendly Salmon Crackers

Contributed by Kyarii Ramarui

Ingredients
Tzatziki
Smoked Salmon Slices
Capers
Lemon
Ritz Crackers
Dill *optional*

Instructions
Lay out as many Ritz crackers as desired on a plate. Spread about a teaspoon of tzatziki onto each Ritz cracker. Place one to two slices of smoked salmon onto each cracker. (If the salmon is not already sliced, slice it into square inch pieces for easy layering). Place a few capers on top of the salmon. For a tangier taste, add a few drops of lemon juice to each cracker and adorn with a sprig of dill.

Hot Crab Dip

Contributed by Kelsey Lang

Ingredients
2 - 8oz blocks of cream cheese
1/2 pint sour cream
3 teaspoon Worcestershire sauce
1 ½ teaspoon dry mustard
3 tablespoons mayonnaise
½ teaspoon garlic powder
1 lemon, juiced
1 tablespoon old bay seasoning
1 pound crab meat
Sharp Cheese

Instructions
Mix all the ingredients except the cheese in a large bowl. Place mixture in a baking dish. Bake for 15 minutes at 350 degrees. Remove it from the oven and sprinkle with the Sharp Cheese. Bake for another 15 minutes.

Spinach Dip

Contributed by Katharine Shaver

Ingredients
3 packages of frozen spinach
1 cup mayonnaise
1 cup sour cream
1 package of vegetable soup mix
1 round ball type bread - any kind

Instructions
Hollow bread, cube the remaining. Prepare spinach according to package, drain. Add all ingredients in a bowl, mix. Spoon into bread and arrange remaining cubes around the loaf. Refrigerate about 1 hour before serving.

"This is my advice to people: Learn how to cook, try new recipes, learn from your mistakes, be fearless, and above all have fun"

~ Julia Child

ഔ SIDE DISHES ക

Cheeseburger Rice

Contributed by Kathleen Britt

Ingredients
1 pound ground beef
1 cup ketchup
½ cup water
2 tablespoon mustard
4 oz shredded cheddar cheese
1 ½ cup Minute Rice
Onions *optional*
Garlic *optional*

Instructions
Begin by browning the ground beef in a frying pan. If chosen to use onions and garlic, add that to the pan with the ground beef to cook. Next, add the ketchup, water, and mustard, and bring to a slow boil. Add the rice, remove from the heat, and cover. Let it stand for five to seven minutes. Quickly remove the cover, and add the cheese. Again, let stand for two to three minutes. Mix and serve.

Balsamic Roasted Red Onion

Contributed by Elaine Yang

Ingredients
1 medium to large red onion
1 teaspoon of canola (or olive oil)
¼ cup of balsamic vinegar

Instructions
Preheat the oven to 450 degrees. Cut the red onion into small wedges. In a pan, heat the oil of choice. On medium heat, pan-fry the onions for 3-5 minutes. Put the onions on a cookie sheet. Pour the balsamic vinegar on the onions. Bake the onions in the oven for 10 minutes until the vinegar has been fully soaked in. Take out the onions and serve.

Squash Casserole

Contributed by Meghan Cusack

Ingredients
2 zucchini squash
2 yellow squash
½ onion
1 can cream of chicken soup
½ cup grated cheddar cheese
1 stick butter
1 box stove top stuffing

Instructions

Boil, squash with chopped onion for 5 minutes drain. Mix vegetables together cream of chicken soup and sour cream. Melt ½ stick butter and combine with seasoning packet from stove top stuffing, combine with dressing and put a layer in the bottom a 12 by 12 inch the baking dish, spoon in the squash mixture sprinkle with grated cheddar cheese and cover with the remainder of the dressing. Bake at 350° for 30 minutes or until bubbly.

Vic's Famous Chow-Chow

Contributed by Ashley Porter

Ingredients

25 tomatoes
2-3 onions
1 dozen Spanish peppers (or 2 jalapenos, seeded)
½ cup kosher salt

Instructions

Grind tomatoes, onions, and jalapenos in a food processor. Mix in kosher salt. Transfer to glass or ceramic container, letting it sit for 2 or 3 days. Taste to see if sour, add more salt if it is not sour enough. Transfer mixture to pickling jars, and store in refrigerator.

Filipino Egg Rolls (Lumpia)

Contributed by Ashley Porter

Ingredients
2 pounds ground pork or beef
1 ½ cups carrots, grated
1 ½ medium onion, diced
1 ½ cups celery, diced
2 cloves garlic, minced
1 cup green onion, chopped
1 teaspoon black pepper
1 package spring roll wrappers
1 egg, separated
Oil for frying
1 jar sweet and sour sauce

Instructions
Heat enough oil in a skillet for frying.
Separate egg yolk from egg white, setting aside egg white in a bowl. Combine meat, carrots, onion, celery, garlic, green onion, pepper, and egg yolk in a large bowl until it is evenly mixed.

Lay one spring roll wrapper on a flat surface. Add meat filling in a straight line across the wrapper. Roll the meat filling in the wrapper (like you would with a burrito). Seal the roll, using the egg white to seal down the ending flap of the spring roll wrapper. Repeat this until spring roll wrappers are gone. Fry in the oil, flipping halfway through, until rolls are a golden brown. Serve with sweet and sour sauce on side.

Meatless Option:
Replace meat with shredded, boiled cabbage.

Chicken Fried Rice

Contributed by Vanessa Beruetta

Ingredients
¼ pound of chicken
1 cup of rice
2 tablespoons sesame oil
½ small white onion, chopped
1 cup frozen peas and carrots, thawed
Soy sauce (more or less to taste)
2 eggs, lightly beaten
2 tablespoon chopped green onions (optional)
1 head broccoli

Instructions
Lightly grease pan with vegetable oil. Cook onions, peas, carrots, and eggs together. Add green onions. After 5 minutes, add rice, stir rice in, on low heat, and add broccoli. Mix in already cooked chicken, add soy sauce to taste.

Korean Fried Rice

Contributed by Grace Choung

Ingredients

5 cups of cooked fried rice
2 to 3 cups of vegetables (such as carrots, green beans, green peas, or yellow corn)
1 cup of onion
1 can of spam (diced into small cubes) *can be substituted with sausage or shrimp*
1 teaspoon salt
1 teaspoon black pepper
1 ½ tablespoons olive oil
1 to 2 teaspoon sesame seed oil
½ cup roasted sesame seeds

Instructions

Begin by stir frying the vegetables with ½ tablespoon olive oil and ½ teaspoon salt and black pepper. Set aside. Next, stir fry the diced onions with ½ tablespoon olive oil. Then set it off to the side as well. Continue by stir frying choice of meat with ½ tablespoon olive oil. Add the vegetables and onions in with the Spam, and also add the cooked rice. As you stir them together, add the sesame seed oil and the sesame seeds. Add to this mix the rest of the salt and black pepper and continue stirring until it is well mixed. Serve.

Spanish Rice

Contributed by Shelby Galow

Ingredients
2 to 3 tablespoons butter or margarine
1 ½ cups long grain rice
2 small cans of tomato paste
Garlic salt
Seasoning salt
Onion salt
Salt
Pepper
Caldo de pollo (Chicken Bouillon)
2 cups of Water

Instructions
In a large saucepan, on medium high heat, melt butter or margarine. Then pour half the bag of rice into the sauce pan. Let rice sit for around 10 minutes, stirring occasionally, until rice has browned. Add water to cover the rice. Add the tomato paste, and the remaining seasonings to taste. Let stand, stirring occasionally until the mixture comes to a boil. Cover and simmer for about fifteen minutes. Turn the heat down to medium low and stir halfway through. When the rice is fluffy and all the water has evaporated, remove from the heat and serve.

Fried Buttery Potatoes

Contributed by: Soobin Ahn

Ingredients
10 baby potatoes (about 10 oz)
2 1/3 cups water
1 teaspoon salt
2 tablespoon butter
Parsley leaves (for optional garnishing)

Instructions
Prepare 10 baby potatoes by peeling them and keeping them in cold water to prevent browning. In a pan, add the water, potatoes, and salt. Bring the water to a boil, and cook the potatoes for 15 to 20 mins on high. Potatoes will be ready when a fork can smoothly pierce the potatoes. Drain any leftover water. Next, melt the butter in a pan. Add the cooked potatoes into the heated pan, and fry them on medium-low. It is important not to fry them on high, or they will not absorb the buttery flavor before burning. Turn them occasionally, until the potatoes become evenly browned. If you choose to use parsley, sprinkle on the finished potatoes.

Cucumber Raita

Contributed by Mukta Joshi

Ingredients
2 cucumbers, finely chopped
3 cups plain yogurt
1 green chili, finely chopped
Salt, to taste
Sugar, to taste
½ cup peanuts, crushed
6 mint leaves, finely chopped
⅓ cup cilantro, finely chopped

Instructions
Mix all the ingredients together and refrigerator for one hour before serving.

"Simple ingredients, treated with respect... put them together and you will always have a great dish."
~ Jose Andres Puerta

℘ BREAKFAST ℘

Apple Pancakes

Contributed by Meghan Thomas

Ingredients
2 cups flour
3 teaspoon baking powder
1 teaspoon salt
2 tablespoon sugar
1 teaspoon cinnamon
1 egg
1 ½ cups milk
3 tablespoon melted butter
1 cup finely chopped apple

Instructions
Combine flour, baking powder, salt, sugar, and cinnamon in a bowl. Add egg, milk, and melted butter. Mix thoroughly. Stir in the chopped apple to the batter. On a skillet, place approximately a spoonful of the batter. Flip the pancake after the edges slightly harden and bubbles begin to form on top of the batter. Cook until golden brown.

Brunch Frittata

Contributed by Christina Smith

Ingredients
8 eggs
½ cup milk
2 tablespoon olive oil
½ pound sliced mushrooms
2 cups raw spinach
½ stick (¼ cup) of butter
½ cup Swiss cheese
Salt and pepper

Instructions
Mix eggs and milk in bowl with a wire whisk. Add olive oil to a skillet with sliced mushrooms and spinach. Sauté until mushrooms are soft and spinach is wilted. In a non-stick skillet, add butter and melt over medium heat. Add egg/milk mixture and allow the eggs to set. While eggs are still cooking, add spinach/mushroom mixture. Cover skillet until eggs are hard. Add Swiss cheese and allow it to melt on top of the egg. Salt and pepper to desired flavor. Cut in wedges and serve with a slice of bread.

Classic French Toast

Contributed by Grace Choung

Ingredients

6 slices of bread
4 eggs
¼ cup of milk
Butter
Dash of salt
Maple syrup
Sugar powder
Fruit (strawberries, blueberries, etc)

Instructions

In a wide bowl, crack 4 eggs and beat lightly with a fork. Stir in milk and salt. Heat up a pan on medium heat and butter the pan lightly. One at a time, place the slices of bread into the mixture so it soaks it up on both sides. Slowly transfer each slice to the pan. Heat until golden brown and then brown the other side. Serve with a light layer of sugar powder, cut up fruit, and warm maple syrup.

Baked French Toast

Contributed by Meghan Cusack

Ingredients
¼ to ½ cups sugar or Splenda
2 cups milk
8 - 10 eggs (or 2 ½ cups egg beaters)
2 teaspoon vanilla
16 oz cream cheese cut in small chunks
1 loaf bread (crusts can be removed if desired)
1 inch pieces
½ teaspoon nutmeg

Instructions
Mix eggs, sugar nutmeg and vanilla in a
separate bowl and set aside
Spray bottom of 9 X 13 pan and layer ½ the
bread on the bottom. Spread the cream
cheese on the bread layer (small chunks),
cover with the remaining bread and pour the
egg mixture over the top. Cover and
refrigerate overnight. Dust with nutmeg, bake
at 375° for 45 to 50 minutes until the top is
nicely browned. Serve with your favorite
flavored syrups. Ideal for a large group or a
holiday morning.

Fat-free Vegan Blueberry Pancakes

Contributed by Sayre Posey

Ingredients
1/2 cup blueberries
1/3 cup whole wheat
2 tablespoons rolled oats
1/2 teaspoon cinnamon
2/3 teaspoon baking powder
1/8 teaspoon salt
1/2 teaspoon pure vanilla extract
1 tablespoon sugar
1/3 cup milk

Instructions
Mix the whole wheat, rolled oats, cinnamon, baking powder, salt, and sugar together. Add pure vanilla extract and milk until lumps disappear. Spray a pan, pour two tablespoons of the batter at a time on the pan, and cook on low-medium heat. Flip the pancakes when the top starts to bubble. Cook until golden brown, and serve.

Sticky Buns

Contributed by Meghan Cusack

Ingredients
3 ½ oz package uncooked butterscotch
  pudding (not instant)
1 cup chopped pecans
2 dozen frozen Parker house style rolls
½ cup sugar
1 teaspoon cinnamon
½ cup butter
½ cup brown sugar packed

Instructions
Grease a 9 by 13 pan (Clean up is easier if you
line the pan with baking parchment, greasing
both sides). Sprinkle pudding mix in bottom,
spread on the nuts. Put rolls over the nuts so
that they don't touch each other. Mix
cinnamon and sugar and sprinkle over the
rolls. Melt butter and brown sugar and drizzle
over all. Cover with tented foil and let rise
over night. Bake at 350° for 30 minutes.
Turn out onto a cookie sheet, enjoy warm.

Fluffy White Chocolate Chip Waffles with Homemade Strawberry Sauce

Contributed by Vanessa Hall

Ingredients
2 eggs
2 ½ cup bread flour *substitute could be all-
   purpose flour*
4 tablespoons baking powder
½ tablespoon baking soda
1 tablespoon sugar
¼ teaspoon salt
1 ¾ cup milk
½ cup vegetable oil
½ teaspoon vanilla extract
½ cup white chocolate chips
½ cup strawberries
½ cup agave nectar

Instructions
Place the uncracked eggs in a bowl of warm water and let sit until room temperature. Crack the eggs into a bowl and whisk until fluffy. In the same bowl with the eggs, mix in the salt, milk, vegetable oil, vanilla extract, and sugar. Whisk until everything is combined and fluffy. In a separate bowl, combine the bread flour, baking soda, and baking powder. Mix

until everything is evenly distributed. Add the wet ingredients to the dry ingredients and whisk until smooth. Add the white chocolate chips to the batter, and whisk until evenly distributed throughout. Pour the batter into a waffle griddle. For the sauce, dice the fresh strawberries and place them in a hot pot. Stir them around until soft. Add the agave nectar to the pot. Mix until the sauce starts to gently bubble. Lightly drizzle over the prepared waffle and serve.

Sausage Gravy and Biscuits

Contributed by Ashley Porter

Ingredients
½ package mild sausage
2 tablespoon butter
2 tablespoon all-purpose flour
5 cups milk
1 ½ teaspoon salt
1 ½ teaspoon pepper

Instructions
Cook sausage until done. Add butter and flour. Simmer for a few minutes on medium heat, stirring frequently. Add milk, salt, and pepper. Simmer over medium heat, stirring constantly until desired thickness. Serve over top of cooked store-bought flaky biscuits.

South Asian Omelet

Contributed by Archana Nilaweera

Ingredients

2 eggs
½ of an onion
1 green chili pepper
Pepper
Salt
Maldive fish flakes
Diced tomatoes
1 tablespoon olive oil

Instructions

Cut the pepper, onion, and tomatoes into small pieces. In a bowl, beat the eggs, pepper, onions, tomatoes, and Maldive fish flakes with a fork. Heat a skillet with the olive oil, and after the skillet is hot, pour the egg mixture into the skillet. Let the mixture cook, and midway through cooking the omelet, fold the egg in half. Cook until the consistency is no longer runny. Remove the skillet from the heat and serve.

"All happiness depends on a leisurely breakfast."
~ John Gunther

ஓ LUNCH ௸

Hotdogs With a Kick

Contributed by Archana Nilaweera

Ingredients
8 hotdogs *can substitute with Italian
    sausages*
1 medium onion *optional*
Salt
Black Pepper
Ketchup
1 tablespoon olive oil

Instructions
Begin by boiling the hotdogs until they are
cooked. Heat a small amount of olive oil in a
skillet. Cut the hotdogs into small pieces and
slightly fry them in the skillet until they are
golden brown. Next, cut the onions into a
desired size, and add them to the skillet.
Sprinkle a desired amount of salt and pepper
on the hotdogs and onions, and mix in a
desired amount of ketchup. Heat the mixture
in the skillet for about three minutes until
warm. Remove from the stove and serve.

Egg and Mayo Sandwich

Contributed by Muskan Pathak

Ingredients
2 eggs
Salt and Pepper (Optional)
2 tablespoons of mayo
2 slices of your choice of bread

Instructions
Place eggs in a saucepan full of cold. Make sure eggs are fully covered by water. Boil the eggs on HIGH heat on the stove. Drain water immediately and let the eggs cool. Remove shell from eggs and completely mash up the eggs in a bowl. Add in mayo. Mix well. Add salt and pepper as desired. (optional) Place the egg and mayo mix a slice of bread and create sandwich. Enjoy!

Italian Grilled Cheese

Contributed by Trinh Hoang

Ingredients
2 slices of Italian bread
Grilled chicken (optional)
1/4 cup unsalted butter
2 tablespoon basil pesto
2 slices of fresh mozzarella

Instructions

Begin by spreading the pesto on both slices of bread. Add the mozzarella and grilled chicken onto the bread. In a small skillet, on medium heat, add butter, and heat until it is melted. Add the sandwich to skillet to grill. Flip the sandwich regularly, and cook until the cheese is fully melted.

Pizza Pockets

Contributed by Ashley Porter

Ingredients

1 package refrigerated flaky biscuits
1 small jar pizza sauce
1 package mozzarella cheese
Pepperoni, bacon, onion, any other pizza
   toppings *optional*

Instructions

Preheat oven to 400 degrees. Press each biscuit into a 5 inch circle. Spread about 1 tablespoon sauce over half of the circle, keeping it about a half inch away from the edge. Sprinkle about 1-2 tablespoons of cheese. Add toppings, if wanted. Fold circle in half and press edges with a fork to seal. Place on nonstick (or greased) cookie sheet and bake 12-15 minutes, or until golden brown.

Spinach and Tuna Sandwich

Contributed by Elaine Yang

Ingredients
7 cups of broken up bread
Fresh spinach
2 eggs
4 egg whites
½ cup of walnuts
1 onion, diced
salt and black pepper
3 slices of garlic
1 serving spoon of dill
1 serving spoon of chopped up celery
Canned tuna
Sliced apple
Yellow mustard

Instructions
Preheat the oven to 375. Wash spinach and make sure it's dry. Whisk the eggs fully. Put the 7 cups of bread into a bowl and mix with mixer. Add all ingredients and mix well. Put mixture in a greased metal bread mold. Bake for 30 minutes. After 30 minutes, set the mixture aside to cool for 15 minutes. Slice the bread. Mix the dill, tuna, apple pieces, mustard and mayo. Put the desired amount of tuna in the bread and serve.

ಠ DINNER ಜ

Angel Chicken

Contributed by Erin O'Sullivan

Ingredients
9 or more chicken breast halves
¼ cup butter or margarine
2 - 7ounce envelopes of Italian dry salad
  dressing mix
2 - 10 3/4 ounce cans condensed golden
  mushroom soup
1 - 8 ounce tub cream cheese w chives &
  onions
1 cup water

Instructions
Put chicken in crockpot. In medium sauce
pan melt butter, salad dressing mix,
mushroom soup, cream cheese and water.
Pour over chicken. Cook 5 + hours on low.
Serve over angel hair pasta.
Can be slow cooked in the oven at 350
degrees for 1 hour or until chicken breasts are
tender.

Beef Cheesearoni

Contributed by Ashley Porter

Ingredients
1 pound ground beef
1 ½ teaspoon garlic salt
1 medium onion, sliced
1 28 ounce can tomatoes
1 6 ounce can tomato paste
1/2 teaspoon oregano
½ teaspoon basil
1 ½ teaspoon chili powder
6 ounce large uncooked macaroni
1 16 ounce container low fat cottage cheese
1 cup mozzarella cheese
3 tablespoon Romano cheese

Instructions
Season ground beef with garlic salt. Spread in shallow nonstick pan or broiler pan. Broil meat about 2 inches from heat until surface is brown. Drain off fat.

Combine meat. onion, tomatoes, tomato paste, oregano, basil and chili powder in a pan. Bring to a boil. Cover and reduce to low heat, simmering for 1 hour and stirring frequently until sauce is thicker. Cook and drain macaroni. Toss drained macaroni with cottage cheese. Spread macaroni mixture at the bottom of a pan. Top with mozzarella, sauce mixture, romano cheese. Wrap tightly with foil and bake at 325 degrees for 1 hour, or until bubbly. (Can also be frozen and baked later!)

Coffee Rubbed Beef Tenderloin

Contributed by Emily Bordenski

Ingredients

1½ pound of beef tenderloin steaks
¼ cup instant espresso powder
1 tablespoon ground cumin
1 tablespoon garlic salt
1 tablespoon paprika
Butter

Instructions

Preheat oven to 400 degrees. Combine all ingredients and coat steaks with the mixture all over. Melt butter in a pan over medium-high heat and sear the steaks on all sides. Finish the steaks in the oven to a desired wellness.

Beef Kimbap (Korean Sushi)

Contributed by: Soobin Ahn

Ingredients

10 sheets of dried seaweed
1 cup of ground beef
9 oz spinach (1/2 cup boiled spinach)
20 pieces burdock root
10 pieces pickled radish
1 cup carrot
5 eggs
7-8 bowls of cooked short grain or sushi rice
1 green onion
1 tablespoon garlic
1 1/2 tablespoons soy sauce
1 tablespoon sugar
1/2 tablespoon cooking wine
1/8 teaspoon black pepper
1 teaspoon salt
1 1/2 tablespoon and 1 teaspoon sesame oil
1 1/2 tablespoon olive oil
1/2 tablespoon sesame seeds
Servings: About 10 rolls

Instructions

In a bowl combine ground beef, green onion, garlic, soy sauce, sugar, cooking wine, 1 ½ tablespoon sesame oil, and black pepper. Thoroughly mix together and set aside.

In boiling water, add the spinach and a pinch of salt. Boil for thirty seconds to one minute. Rinse the spinach in cold water and squeeze out the excess water. Next, mix together the boiled spinach, 1/2 teaspoon of sesame oil, and 2 pinches of salt. In a separate bowl mix together the eggs and 5 pinches of salt.

In a pan, on medium heat, add a little oil and spread it around. Then, pour the egg mixture into the pan and cook until the surface is no longer runny. Reduce the temperature to low and flip the egg over. Continue to fry it until both sides of the egg are thoroughly cooked. Afterwards, cut the egg into half-inch strips and cut the pickled radish into half-inch strips. Julienne the carrot thinly. Fry the carrot in a little cooking oil and salt on medium heat until cooked. Prepare about 10 pieces of seasoned burdock.

Next, fry the marinated beef until completely cooked. In a large bowl, add the cooked rice, 1 1/2 tablespoon of sesame oil, olive oil, 1 teaspoon of salt, and sesame seeds. Mix gently, so your rice will not become mashed. Then, cover the rice with plastic wrap so it will not dry out.

Place a sheet of dried seaweed on a bamboo mat. The shiny part of the seaweed sheet should be on the bottom. Spread some rice across two thirds of the seaweed sheet. On top of the rice, place the burdock, egg, carrot, spinach, beef, and pickled radish. Tightly roll the seaweed sheet. Place some rice on the end of the seaweed sheet to seal it shut. Roll the kimbap with the bamboo mat or parchment paper and squeeze it hard to shape it. Spread sesame oil on the surface of the kimbap. Finish by cutting the roll into half inch pieces or bite sized pieces.

Cheese Enchiladas

Contributed by Shelby Galow

Ingredients
1 block sharp cheddar cheese
1 block Monterey jack cheese
1 30 count package corn tortillas
1 large and 1 small can of enchilada sauce
¼ cup vegetable or olive oil

Instructions
Preheat oven to 200 degrees. Grate the blocks of cheddar and Monterey jack cheese and combine them in a large bowl. Set aside. On low, in separate saucepans, heat the vegetable

oil and the enchilada sauce, and warm for a few minutes. Place one corn tortilla in the oil to warm. Using tongs, pull the tortilla out, and let the excess oil drip off. Immediately place the tortilla in the enchilada sauce. Again, using tongs, pull the tortilla out of the enchilada sauce and place it on a small salad plate. Place a handful of cheese in the middle of the tortilla. Roll the tortilla and place it on a baking sheet with the end of the tortilla facing down.

Repeat these steps until you have finished the pack of tortillas. As you use the enchilada sauce, add more to the pan in order to coat each tortilla evenly. Once you have finished the pack of tortillas, take any excess sauce and pour it over the tortillas on the baking sheet. Sprinkle cheese over the top of the enchiladas. Place enchiladas in the oven for 15 to 20 minutes. Serve warm.

"Cheese. Milk's leap toward immortality"
~ Clifton Fadiman

Chicken Tikka

Contributed by Mukta Joshi

Ingredients
1 pound boneless chicken
½ tablespoon tandoori chicken masala (store bought – from Indian grocery store)
1 tablespoon ginger garlic paste
1 tablespoon coriander powder *optional*
Salt to taste
2 tablespoon plain yogurt
1 tablespoon canola, olive, or vegetable oil
1 onion *optional*
1 green pepper *optional*
Half lemon for serving *optional*

Instructions
Mix all the spices, salt and ginger garlic paste in yogurt well and remove all lumps. Cut chicken in to small pieces. Mix chicken pieces and the yogurt mixture. Marinate chicken in refrigerator for minimum 4 hours (or overnight for more tender tikkas). Add oil in the chicken just before grilling. Grill the chicken on skewers or cook it in a hot pan for about 6 to 8 minutes or until cooked. Serve hot with grilled onion and green peppers. Squeeze lemon on chicken before serving (optional).

Omurice

Contributed by Julie Doan

Ingredients
Vegetable oil
¼ onion
½ a teaspoon minced garlic
4 button mushrooms
frozen peas
⅓ pound of chicken breast (any meat is fine)
4 eggs
Milk
Salt & Pepper
Ketchup
Oyster sauce (Hoisin sauce also works)
½ pound steamed, white rice

Instructions
Fry the onions, garlic, mushrooms, thawed peas and chicken. Add rice and mix. Gradually add ketchup according to taste. Add half a teaspoon of oyster sauce. Mix well...but don't break the rice grains or everything will be mushy. Adjust the taste with salt and pepper. Put onto a separate plate and form a dome with the rice. Mix the 4 eggs with salt, pepper, and milk in a bowl. Fry the mixture to make an omelet. Flip the omelet onto the rice. Garnish with some ketchup on top.

Creole Style Gumbo

Contributed by Vanessa Hall

Ingredients

1 16 ounce packages frozen diced okra
1 large onions, diced
1 large green peppers, diced
1/2 pound of large frozen shrimp
1/2 pound of large sea scallops
1/2 pound of large diced cod fish
1 cups celery, diced
3 28 ounce cans Contadina whole tomatoes
1/2 medium garlic bulb
3 bay leaves
Salt to taste
Black pepper to taste
Ground cayenne pepper to taste
1 6-ounce cans Hunts tomato paste
1 14.5-ounce cans stewed tomatoes (onion, celery, green pepper)

Instructions

In a large pot, cook down half a package of okra; until it turns brown. Cook down onions and green peppers. Set aside. Add garlic onions and green peppers to okra. Boil a small pot of water then turn the heat off. Add shrimp to the water for five minutes; pour the water out of pot, and season the shrimp with hot sauce and salt. Set shrimp aside. Add the following to all of the above, except for the shrimp: Squeezed the whole tomatoes, stewed tomatoes, and diced tomatoes; Add to the pot. Fill ¾ of the pot with water. Add the diced celery and bay leaves. Slow cook for half an hour. Add codfish and the other half package of okra. Cook until the okra slimes surface. The pot should be hot. Add sea scallops, shrimp, and two cans of Hunt's tomatoes. Cook on low heat for five minutes and LETS EAT.

Slow Cooker Sloppy Joes

Contributed by Meghan Cusack

Ingredients
2 pounds ground beef
1 ½ cup chopped onions
¾ cup chili sauce
½ cup water
¼ cup mustard
2 rounded teaspoons chili powder.

Instructions
Brown beef and onions. Drain off the fat. Pour all into a slow cooker and cook on low for 6 hours. Serve on hamburger rolls with coleslaw.

Ed's Spicy Chili

Contributed by Emily Murphy

Ingredients
2 pounds top sirloin steak, cubed
2 pounds lean ground beef
1 large yellow onion, chopped
28 oz can peeled whole tomatoes, undrained
32 oz beef broth
¼ cup chili powder
1 cinnamon stick
1 teaspoon garlic salt
2 teaspoon cumin
1 teaspoon dried basil
3 bay leaves
2 jalapenos
1 teaspoon yellow cornmeal
2 tablespoons light olive oil
Salt
Pepper

Instructions
Place the olive oil in large stockpot over medium heat. Brown sirloin in batches. Remove meat from the heat to a large bowl. Add ground beef and the onion to the pot to brown, breaking up the beef into small pieces. Return the sirloin, with the drippings, to pot. Add all of the remaining ingredients. Bring

this to a boil, and then reduce to a simmer. Simmer for 2 or more hours, breaking up the tomatoes and ground beef and skimming grease. Remove the cinnamon stick, bay leaves, and jalapenos before serving. Serve with grated cheddar cheese, sour cream, and warm bread. Can also be served over hot rice.

Kona Chicken

Contributed by Ashley Porter

Ingredients
3 pounds Chicken Breast
¾ cup Green Onion, Chopped
½ cup Soy Sauce
¼ cup White Wine
½ cup Water
½ cup Honey
1 tablespoon oil

Instructions
Brown chicken in a skillet using oil. Mix together onion, soy sauce, wine, and water. Pour mixture on top of chicken in slow cooker. Cover and cook on low for approximately 3-5 hours (or until tender). Remove chicken and brush with honey and place in broiler. Continue brushing with honey until chicken is a golden brown color. Serve with sauce from slow cooker.

Green Beans and Beef Stir Fry

Contributed by Trinh Hoang

Ingredients

2 tablespoon vegetable oil
2 cloves of garlic minced
2 cups green beans washed
1 pound sirloin tips thinly sliced
4 tablespoon oyster sauce
1/2 onion sliced
1/4 cup of water
Salt and Pepper for seasoning

Instructions

In a large skillet, heat 1 tablespoon of vegetable oil for one minute on high heat. Add 1 clove of minced garlic to the skillet and turn down to medium heat, add meat. Cook until brown (about 2 minutes). Transfer cooked sirloin tips to a large bowl, and set aside. Add 1 tablespoon of oil and the second clove of minced garlic into the skillet. Add the onions, and cook until they are translucent. Next, add the green beans and water. Cover the skillet and simmer for 4 minutes. Stir in the beef and oyster sauce. Cook for an additional 2 minutes, stirring constantly. Remove from heat, and serve with white or brown rice (optional).

Harvest Spaghetti

Contributed by Christina Smith

Ingredients
Box of spaghetti noodles
2 tablespoons olive oil
2 teaspoons minced garlic
1 onion
2 cups kale
1 zucchini
2 fresh tomatoes
Jar of plain spaghetti sauce
½ cup pine nuts
Parmesan cheese (optional)

Instructions
Boil spaghetti noodles in accordance with package directions. Add to a skillet the olive oil and garlic. Chop onion and zucchini and add both. Sauté both over medium heat until brown and soft. Add kale and sauté over medium heat until wilted. Add spaghetti sauce and simmer for 10 minutes. Toast pine nuts in oven at 325 degrees until brown. Drain spaghetti and pour the sauce over it. Add pine nuts and fresh grated parmesan cheese if desired.

Latino-Inspired Lasagna

Contributed by Ingrid DePaz

Ingredients
1 onion, diced
1/3 cup butter
1/3 cup flour
1 cup skim milk
2 cups chicken broth
2 cups shredded cheese of your choice
1 pound ground beef
7 chorizo peppers
6 ripened plantains
2 tablespoons cumin
2 tablespoons Worcestershire sauce
2 lemons, squeezed
1 teaspoon paprika
1 teaspoon oregano

Instructions
Preheat oven to 350 F. Grease a 9" by 13" pan. Melt the butter in a saucepan and add the onions. Add salt and pepper to taste. Cook on low heat until transparent. Mix in flour and cumin and cook for 1 minute. Gradually add broth and stir. Add milk. Continue stirring until the sauce has thickened. Once the sauce has thickened, add 1 cup of the cheese. Stir until melted. Transfer the sauce to a bowl and

cover. In a large skillet, cook the chorizos until browned, breaking down large pieces. Once cooked, add the ground beef and cook until brown, breaking down large pieces. Drain the oil. Add Worcestershire sauce, lemon, and oregano. Season with salt and pepper to taste. Cut plantains in halves and peel. Cut each half lengthwise three times. Layer the pan with plantains. Then layer the meats on top. Add a layer of the cheese sauce. Make sure each layer is spread out evenly. Continue adding layers of plantains, meats, and cheese sauce. Once the last layer of plantain has been added, layer with remaining cup of shredded cheese. Sprinkle paprika over the cheese evenly. Cook for 1 hour.

"One cannot think well, love well, sleep well, if one has not dined well."
~ Virginia Woolf

Lomo Saltado

Contributed by Emily Diaz

Ingredients
1 pound beef
2 onions
1 tomato
1 tablespoon chopped garlic
Pepper
Cumin
Salt
Vinegar
Soy sauce
Vegetable oil

Instructions
Cut beef into one inch thick slices. Place in skillet with a little vegetable oil. Fry beef, add pepper, cumin, garlic and let it cook. Add cut up onions and add some vinegar until the onions are almost transparent. Add soy sauce and then tomatoes cut just like the onions. Add some water if you like to dilute the flavor and have some extra sauce. Serve with French fries and white rice.

Microwave Pasta Dish

Contributed by Anlara McKenzie

Ingredients
Pasta
Water
Tomatoes
Scallions
Parmesan cheese
Parsley
Oregano

Instructions
Place the uncooked pasta in a microwavable bowl, and fill it with enough water to cover the pasta. Cook in the microwave for four to six minutes, or until the pasta is at a desired texture. Drain the pasta. Add diced tomatoes, chopped scallions, shredded Parmesan cheese, and a dash of parsley and oregano. Mix and cook for one to two minutes in the microwave, or until the cheese is melted.

Papa a la Huancaina

Contributed by Emily Diaz

Ingredients
Cream cheese
Evaporated milk
1 egg*
Vegetable oil
1 tablespoon Peruvian Aji Amarillo (yellow
  chili pepper from Peru Paste)
Pepper
Salt
Lemon

Instructions
Blend milk, cream cheese and chili paste in a
blender. Add pepper, salt, a little oil, egg, and
about a fourth of the lemon juice in the lemon
and blend some more. Served with cooked
potatoes and lettuce.

*Publishers note: Consuming raw or
undercooked meats, poultry, seafood,
shellfish, or eggs may increase your risk of
foodborne illness, especially if you have a
medical condition.

Roast Turkey

Contributed by Kristina Cronise

Ingredients
1 (15 to 18 pound) turkey fresh or thawed

Brine:
1 cup kosher salt
1/3 cup brown sugar
1 gallon vegetable stock
3 cups apple juice/apple cider
1 tablespoon black peppercorns
1 teaspoon allspice berries
1 teaspoon chopped candied ginger
1 gallon ice water

Aromatics:
1 apple, sliced
½ onion, sliced
1 cinnamon stick
1 cup water
4 rosemary sprigs
6 sage leaves
Canola oil

Instructions
Make brine the day before roasting. Combine the vegetable stock, apple juice, salt, brown sugar, peppercorns, allspice berries, and

candied ginger in a large pot. Bring to a boil. When the salt and sugar are dissolved, remove from heat, cool and refrigerate.

On the night before roasting, combine the brine, water and ice in a 5-gallon container. Remove the neck and giblet packet from the thawed turkey and put it side down in brine. If necessary, weigh down the bird to ensure it is fully immersed, cover, and refrigerate or set in cool area for 12 to 16 hours. Turn the turkey once halfway through brining.

When you are ready to cook:

Preheat the oven to 450 degrees F. Remove the turkey from the brine, rinse well inside and out with cold water. Discard the brine. Position the bird on roasting rack inside a roasting pan and pat dry with paper towels.

In a microwavable dish, combine the apple, onion, cinnamon stick, and 1 cup of water. Microwave on high for 5 minutes. Water should evaporate and seep into the contents. Put contents into cavity along with the rosemary and sage. Tuck the wings underneath the bird and coat the skin liberally with canola oil.

Cover the breast of the turkey with the foil. Roast the turkey on lowest level of the oven at

450 degrees F for 30 minutes. Then reduce the temperature to 350 degrees. Roast until the thickest part of the breast has reached 165 degrees. A turkey takes approximately 15 minutes per pound to roast, so a 15 to 18 pound bird will require roughly 2 ½ to 3 hours of roasting. However do not rely on time to assess doneness, ALWAYS check the internal temperature with a meat thermometer. When the turkey has finished roasting, remove it from the oven and let it rest, loosely covered with foil for about 15-20 minutes before carving. Pan drippings can be used to make gravy.

"Food, in the end, in our own tradition, is something holy. It's not about nutrients and calories. It's about sharing. It's about honesty. It's about identity."
~ Louise Fresco

Peanut/Coconut Iranian Curry

Contributed by Avanti Mehta

Ingredients
½ cup ground coconut
2 tablespoon peanut butter
3 cups water
¼ cup pasta sauce
3 tablespoon tomato paste
½ teaspoon paprika
1 teaspoon salt
1 teaspoon black pepper
6 hard-boiled eggs, peeled and cooled
1 tablespoon oil
Cilantro *optional*

Instructions
Lightly coat a medium saucepan with oil, and add the ground coconut. Cook on medium-high heat until the coconut is lightly browned. Add the tomato paste and the peanut butter to the coconut, and mix until there is an even consistency. Add the pasta sauce to the pan, and continue cooking on medium heat for about 5 minutes. Add the paprika, salt, and pepper after two to three minutes. Next, add the water and continue cooking on medium heat, stirring frequently. After a few minutes, reduce the heat to low, and cover. Let the mix

simmer for about 15 minutes, stirring occasionally. When the water has reduced enough to leave a slightly thicker consistency, add the hard-boiled eggs and cook on low heat for another 5 to 10 minutes. Garnish with fresh cilantro, and serve.

Leftover Tacos

Contributed by Anlara McKenzie

Ingredients
Corn tortillas
Olive oil
Salt
Salsa
Shredded cheese
Shredded greens (iceberg, romaine or spinach)
Leftover meat (steak, chicken, fish, pork, tofu)

Ingredients
In an iron skillet, heat oil to bubbling and add corn tortilla, fully coating it in oil on both sides. Salt each side to desired taste, and crisp tortilla till golden. Remove from skillet. Heat the leftover meat in skillet until warm. Place meat on tortilla, add salsa, cheese, and greens. Enjoy!
Add avocado slices for an extra treat

Shrimp Creole

Contributed by Katharine Shaver

Ingredients

3 tablespoon olive oil
2 cups celery, chopped
1½ cups bell peppers, chopped
1½ cups onion, chopped
1 large can of tomatoes (1 pound, 12 ounces)
1 small can of tomatoes (1 pound)
1 teaspoon salt and pepper
1 teaspoon thyme leaves
¼ teaspoon garlic powder
3-4 ½ ounce can of shrimp (or 1 pound frozen)
2 tablespoon cornstarch
½ cup of water

Instructions

Put oil in a 4 Quart saucepan. Add celery, bell pepper and onions. Cook slow until tender. Add tomatoes, salt, pepper, thyme, and garlic powder, and simmer for one hour. Thicken with cornstarch. Mixed in cold water, if necessary. Serve on rice.

Slow Cooker Lasagna

Contributed by Ashley Porter

Ingredients

1 pound ground beef or turkey
1 medium onion, diced
1 26 ounce jar spaghetti sauce of choice
12 ounces cottage cheese
Italian herbs of choice (1 teaspoon each of
  basil, oregano, parsley, etc.)
½ cup parmesan cheese, grated
1 egg
12 ounce uncooked lasagna noodles
12 ounce mozzarella, shredded (set aside ½
  cup for topping)

Instructions

Brown meat and drain. Add spaghetti sauce
and simmer until it bubbles (add ½ cup water
to reduce thickness). Combine and
thoroughly mix cottage cheese, parmesan,
mozzarella, Italian herbs, and the egg. Spoon a
layer of meat sauce onto the bottom of
cooker. Add 1 layer of uncooked noodles,
breaking them to fit. Add 1 layer of cheese
mixture. Repeat until all are used. Sprinkle ½
cup of mozzarella on top. Cover and cook on
low for 6-8 hours, or high for 3 hours.

Spaghetti with Meat Sauce

Contributed by Cecilia Grady

Ingredients

2 medium onions
2 medium green peppers
1 1/2 pound ground beef
4 garlic cloves
2 - 28 ounces cans of whole peeled tomatoes
1 14 ounces can tomato sauce
1 - 6 ounces can tomato paste
1 1/4 cups of mushrooms
1 tablespoon dried parsley
1 tablespoon dried basil
2 teaspoons dried oregano
2 teaspoons sugar
1/4 teaspoon thyme
1 teaspoon salt
1 bay leaf
3/4 cup red wine
3/4 cup water

Instructions

Chop onions and peppers. Sauté at medium heat in olive oil until soft. Add the ground beef and garlic, lightly brown. Transfer cooked ground beef mix to a large pot. Add the remaining ingredients, and simmer, uncovered for two to two and a half hours.

Summertime Pasta

Contributed by Julie Vogt

Ingredients
1/3 cup olive oil, plus 1 teaspoon
1/3 cup pine nuts
3 tablespoons red wine vinegar
2 tablespoons capers, chopped
1 clove garlic, finely minced
8 ounces fresh mozzarella cheese, cubed
2½ cups cherry tomatoes, halved
¼ cup red onion, finely minced
½ cup fresh basil, chopped
¼ cup chopped chives
¼ cup chopped parsley
1 teaspoon salt
¼ teaspoon black pepper
12 ounces thin spaghetti

Instructions
Lightly toast pine nuts in pan with 1 teaspoon olive oil, over low heat until light brown, set aside. Cook pasta according to package. Before draining pasta, reserve ¼ cup of cooking water. Add drained pasta to a large skillet with reserved cooking water. Combine remaining ingredients. Mix well, and add to skillet with pasta, then add pine nuts. Mix, warm, and serve.

Vic's Famous Show-Me Chili

Contributed by

Ingredients
2 pounds ground beef
1 large onion, finely chopped
1 celery stalk, finely chopped
2 cans kidney beans
2 cans tomato soup (and 2 cans water)
4 heaping tablespoons chili powder (or less, if desired)
1 can chopped tomatoes (optional)
salt to taste
¼ cup sugar
2 small cans tomato paste (and 2 cans water)

Instructions
Place beef, onion, and celery in a large pot and cook until beef is brown. Add all other ingredients and stir until combined well. Cook on medium high heat until bubbly, then reduce to low heat and simmer for about an hour. Best when served with peanut butter and honey sandwiches for dipping!

White Chili

Contributed by Ashley Porter

Ingredients

1 pound great northern beans, soaked
2 pounds chicken breasts
1 medium onion, chopped
3 cloves garlic, minced
2 4 ounce cans green chilies
2 teaspoon ground cumin
1 teaspoon dried oregano
½ teaspoon salt
1 14.5 ounce can reduced-sodium chicken
  broth
1 cup water

Instructions

Put beans in medium pan and cover with water, bringing to boil. Reduce heat and allow to simmer for 20 minutes. Drain and discard water. Cut chicken into 1-inch pieces and brown if desired. Put all ingredients in slow cooker, stirring to mix thoroughly. Cover and cook on low for 8-10 hours or on high for 4-6 hours.

Baked Chicken & Waffles

Contributed by Yoo-Jin Kang

Ingredients: Serves about 2-3
For the baked chicken:
1 package precooked chicken strips
1 cup greek yogurt (nonfat)
1/4 cup Italian herb breadcrumbs
1 teaspoon garlic powder
1/2 teaspoon cayenne pepper (optional)
1/2 cup grated parmesan cheese

For the Banana Waffles:
1 and 1/2 cup whole wheat flour
2 tablespoons brown sugar
2 teaspoons baking powder
½ teaspoon sea salt
¼ teaspoon cinnamon
1/4 teaspoon nutmeg
⅓ cup melted coconut oil
¾ cup almond milk, warmed (but not hot!)
2 medium and ripened bananas
1 large egg (or flaxseed egg: mix 1 tablespoon
   flaxseed with 3 tablespoons water)
1 teaspoon vanilla extract
Optional: maple syrup for waffles!

Instructions for chicken

Preheat oven to 350 degrees. Line baking tray with parchment paper. Combine garlic powder, parmesan cheese, and optional cayenne pepper with Greek Yogurt. and coat chicken cutlets in the mixture. Afterward, coat the chicken with breadcrumbs (I usually pour the breadcrumbs over the chicken and then flip them over to make sure they're coated). Place coated cutlets on baking tray and bake for 20 minutes (or until golden brown).

Instructions for waffles (need waffle iron)

Preheat waffle iron to the the 2nd hottest or the hottest setting. Combine dry ingredients in a large bowl stir well. Combine wet materials in a separate smaller bowl: make sure the wet materials are well combined (little chunks of banana are okay if you don't mind them in your waffles!). Create a little well in the middle of the dry ingredient bowl. Pour wet ingredients into the dry ingredients and mix until just combined (don't over mix!).

Spray your waffle iron with canola oil spray or even better, coconut oil spray. Pour batter into waffle maker according to your waffle maker's instructions (1/3 cup is usually right).

℀ DESSERTS ℂ

Vanilla Pudding Cake

Contributed by Kelsey Lang

Ingredients
1 box of graham crackers
1-12 ounce package frozen non-dairy whipped
topping thawed
1 large or 2 small packages instant vanilla
pudding
3 ½ cups milk
1 can of chocolate icing

Instructions
Cover the bottom of a 9 x 13 inch pan with
graham crackers. Cut as necessary to make
them fit. Combine pudding mix and milk.
Fold in whipped topping. Spread half of the
pudding mix on top of the graham cracker
layer. Add another layer graham crackers on
top of the pudding. Spread the remaining
pudding mix over the graham crackers. Add a
final layer of graham crackers on top. Spread
chocolate icing over the top. Refrigerate
overnight before serving.

Black Bottom Cupcakes

Contributed by Nicole Magin

Ingredients
1 cup (8oz) cream cheese
1 egg
1/3 cup sugar
1 cup (6 oz) chocolate chips
1 1/2 cups flour
1 cup sugar
1/4 cup cocoa powder
1 teaspoon baking soda
1/2 teaspoon salt
1 cup water
1/3 cup cooking oil
1 tablespoon vinegar
1 teaspoon vanilla

Instructions
Preheat oven to 350 degrees. Combine cream cheese, egg, and 1/3 cup sugar in a small bowl. Beat well and stir in chocolate chips. Set aside. Sift together in a large bowl the flour, 1 cup of sugar, cocoa, baking soda, and sale. Add water, oil, vinegar, and vanilla. Beat until well mixed. Prepare a cupcake pan and fill cups 1/3 of the way full. Top each cup with a heaping teaspoon of the cream cheese mixture. Bake for 25 minutes.

Peach Melba Coffee Cake

Contributed by Kristina Cronise

Ingredients
Crumble Topping and Cake
2 cups all-purpose flour
1 cup granulated sugar
1 teaspoon salt
¾ cup cold unsalted butter (1½ sticks- cut
  into ½ inch pieces)
⅓ cup almonds, slivered
⅓ cup packed light brown sugar
2 teaspoons baking powder
½ cup milk
1 egg
1 teaspoon vanilla extract

Filling
¼ cup water
⅓ cup cornstarch
1 cup sugar
1 teaspoons vanilla extract
1 teaspoon lemon juice
3 cups peeled and chopped peaches (about 1
3/4 pounds)
1½ cups raspberries (6 ounce package)

Topping
¼ cup raspberry preserves

Instructions

Heat oven to 350°F. Coat a 10-inch spring-form pan with nonstick cooking spray.

Topping: In a large bowl, combine flour, sugar and salt. Cut in butter until mixture becomes crumbly. Remove 1 cup of the mixture to a small bowl and stir in the almonds and light brown sugar. Set aside.

Cake: Stir baking powder into the remaining flour mixture. In a small bowl, whisk milk, egg, and vanilla. Stir into the flour mixture until batter forms.

Filling: Mix water, cornstarch, sugar, vanilla extract, and lemon juice in saucepan on medium heat, stir thoroughly. When mixture bubbles, gently fold in fruit, reduce heat to low. If filling is too thick, add more water. If it is too watery, add more cornstarch.

Spoon half batter into prepared pan. Slowly pour filling over it. Drop remaining batter in tablespoons over the fruit and sprinkle with the reserved topping. Bake at 350°F for one hour, until golden-brown and toothpick inserted in the center comes out clean. Cool slightly on wire rack. Run knife around the edge and remove side of pan. Gently heat preserves until melted, drizzle over cake. Serve warm or at room temperature.

Rosemary Shortbread

Contributed by Author Ceci Giltenan

Ingredients

¾ cup salted butter (room temperature)
1 to 1 ½ tablespoons fresh rosemary, finely minced
¾ cup powdered sugar
½ teaspoon vanilla
1 ½ cup flour

Instructions

Cream butter and rosemary well. Add sugar and beat until smooth and a little fluffy. Add vanilla and mix well. Add flour gradually, mixing well between additions. This mixture may be a little crumbly.

If you have a shortbread mold, spray with non-stick coating and press the mixture into the mold. If you don't have a shortbread mold, grease the bottom of a 9 x 9 inch pan (I also line the pan with baking parchment, turning the parchment so both sides are lightly greased) and press the mixture into the prepared pan.

Bake at 325 for 20-25 minutes until just golden brown. Remove from mold or pan while still warm. If using a mold, cut along mold lines while still warm, otherwise cut into squares while still slightly warm. For a 9x9 pan I generally cut either 16 squares or 12 rectangles.

For plain shortbread, omit the rosemary.

Other flavorings such as shredded candied ginger, shredded orange or lemon rind, or other herbs can be used.

Chocolate Quesadillas

Contributed by Sushmitha Kavuru

Ingredients
Pam cooking spray
Tortillas
Chocolate chips (chocolate, white, or other)
Ground cinnamon

Instructions
Take a pan, set it on a low flame, and spray the pan with Pam cooking spray. Place a tortilla on the pan and fold it in half. Open it back up, and on one half, place desired amount of chocolate chips. Fold it back over and press down on it lightly to speed up the melting process. Sprinkle ground cinnamon on top of one side and flip. Let the other half of the tortilla get to a light golden brown, and sprinkle some more cinnamon.

113

Ice Cream Cake

Contributed by Juliana Venegas

Ingredients

4 tablespoons butter
1 package Oreo cookies
1 jar hot fudge topping
½ gallon vanilla ice cream *different flavors
  are optional*
12 ounce cool whip (thawed)

Instructions

Remove the ice cream from freezer and allow
to soften. Crush Oreos into tiny pieces for the
cake crust, using a food processor, blender, or
food chopper. Set aside two to three
tablespoons for the topping. Melt butter and
mix it in with crushed Oreos. Press Oreo
mixture firmly and evenly into the bottom of
a 9" x 13" pan. Place pan in freezer for 15
minutes. Spread half of the ice cream evenly
over the cookie crust. Return pan to freezer
for another 15 minutes. Heat hot fudge in
microwave and drizzle it over first layer of ice
cream. Return pan to freezer for 15 minutes.
Spread remaining ice cream over fudge layer.
Spread cool whip over top like frosting.
Sprinkle with reserved Oreo pieces. Freeze for
at least 4 hours before serving.

Cherry Cheesecake

Contributed by Ashley Porter

Ingredients
2 packages of refrigerated crescent roll dough
1 package of cream cheese
1 can cherry pie filling
2 tablespoon milk
2 cups powdered sugar
1 teaspoon vanilla
1 egg, yolk separated

Instructions
On a circular baking stone or pan, place dough triangles, arranged in a star shape, points meeting in the middle. Flatten slightly. Combine the cream cheese, egg yolk, 1 cup powdered sugar, and vanilla in medium bowl. Mix until fluffy. Spread mixture evenly on dough, leaving spikes of the star shape uncovered. Spread cherry pie filling over mixture, using as little syrup as possible. Pull the spikes of the star over the cream cheese and cherry pie filling, meeting in the middle of the pie. Twist the ends in the middle to hold it together. Bake for 30 minutes on 350 degrees. In a small bowl, mix milk and 1 cup powdered sugar. Once the pie is cool, drizzle this over the pie to create a glaze.

Tres Leches

Contributed by Ingrid DePaz

Ingredients

6 eggs
1 cup sugar
2 cups flour
2 teaspoon baking powder
½ cup milk
1 teaspoon vanilla extract
2 cans condensed milk
1 can evaporated milk
1 cup heavy whipping cream
Cool Whip
Maraschino cherries

Instructions

Preheat oven to 350°F. Separate the egg whites and yolks. Mix the egg whites until they are fluffy. Mix in the egg yolks one at a time. Add the sugar. Separately combine the flour and baking powder. Gradually add the flour mix to the egg and sugar mix while alternating with adding in the ½ cup of milk. Once finished, mix in the vanilla.

Grease a cake pan, pour, and bake for 25 minutes or until golden brown. Let it cool and refrigerate for at least six hours or overnight.

Blend the 3 milks in a blender. Poke holes into the finished cake and pour the blended milk mixture slowly over the cake. Soak the cake in the milk. Spread the Cool Whip evenly over the cake. Add the cherries row by row on top.

Grandma Ann's No Bake Oatmeal Cookies

Contributed by Meghan Herring

Ingredients
½ cup peanut butter
3 cups oatmeal
¼ cup butter or margarine
4 tablespoons cocoa
2 cups sugar
½ cup milk
2 teaspoons vanilla

Instructions
Mix together in a saucepan margarine, cocoa, sugar, milk, and vanilla. Bring to a boil for 3 minutes. Add peanut butter and oatmeal. Mix together. Drop by teaspoons onto waxed paper. Let set.

Eggless Nutella Cupcake

Contributed by Audrey Petrauli

Ingredients
1 teaspoon baking soda
1 ½ teaspoon baking powder
1 cup flour
1 cup 2% milk
1 cup evaporated milk
Sugar (if needed)
3 tablespoon butter, softened
1 jar of Nutella

Instructions
Pour flour into bowl. Sift baking soda and baking powder into the flour mix, then mix it with dry spoon. Pre-heat oven to 375 degrees. Put evaporated milk in a clean bowl, then add 2% milk and butter into the bowl. Mix with hand mixer on medium for 10 seconds. Mix 1/4 of the dry ingredient mix and mix on medium for 10 seconds. Continue doing so until the dry ingredient is all mixed into the wet ingredient. Scoop 2 tablespoons of the batter into cupcake liners. Put 1/3 tablespoon of Nutella into the center of each liner, disperse it so it does not clump in one area. Put in the oven for 20-25 minutes. Decorate with frosting.

Cake Cookies

Contributed by Anlara McKenzie

Ingredients
1 bag of cake mix
2 eggs
½ cup vegetable oil
¼ cup water

Instructions
Combine all ingredients in a large bowl. Beat until smooth. Spoon small amounts of the batter onto an ungreased baking sheet. Bake at 350°F for 8 to 10 minutes.

Grandma Beaulieu's Cake Mix Cookies

Contributed by Meghan Herring

Ingredients
1 package of yellow or white cake mix
1/2 cup of flour
2/3 cup oil
2 eggs
1 cup of chocolate chips

Instructions
Mix together. Drop by spoonful on cookie sheet. Bake at 350°F for 7-9 minutes.

Pumpkin Chiffon Pie

Contributed by Cecilia Grady

Ingredients
2 tablespoons unflavored gelatin mix
1/4 cup cold water
3 eggs
1 cup sugar
1 1/4 cups mashed cooked pumpkin
1/2 teaspoon salt
1/2 teaspoon. ground cinnamon
1/2 teaspoon ground ginger
1/4 teaspoon ground nutmeg
1/2 cup milk
1 pie shell
1 small tub of Cool Whip

Instructions
Add gelatin to cold water, mixing well. Let sit for five minutes. Separate the eggs and beat only the egg yolks, adding 1/2 cup sugar, pumpkin, salt, spices, and milk to the mix. Cook the mixture in a large sauce pan over low/medium heat, stirring constantly until the mix begins to thicken. Add the gelatin to the hot pumpkin mix and stir well. Then, remove it from heat and cool. When the mixture begins to thicken, beat the egg whites until a stiff peak forms. Add the remaining sugar one

tablespoon at a time, beating the mixture in between until the sugar is completely incorporated. Fold the egg whites into the cooled pumpkin mixture with a spatula. Pour the mix into a pie shell and chill until it is firm. Top with cool whip and serve.

Microwave Fudge

Contributed by Meghan Cusack

Ingredients
12 oz chocolate chips
1 can Eagle Brand milk
10 marshmallows halved
¼ cup peanut butter
1 cup walnut pieces

Instructions
Spray a 2 quart microwaveable bowl with vegetable oil spray. Add the chips to the bowl and pour the milk over the chips. Do not stir. Set microwave timer for 5 minutes on high power. Watch for milk to bubble and add the marshmallows on top. Watch and don't allow to boil over. When finished, stir for about 1 minute then add in the peanut butter and nuts. Pour onto a buttered plate and let set overnight uncovered.

Key Lime Fudge

Contributed by Meghan Cusack

Ingredients

3 cup white baking pieces or white chocolate
1 can sweetened condensed milk
2 teaspoon finely shredded lime peel
3 tablespoon key lime juice or regular lime juice
1 cup chopped macadamia nuts, toasted

Instructions

Line an 8-inch square baking pan with foil, extending foil over edges of pan. Butter foil; set aside. In a large heavy saucepan cook and stir baking pieces and sweetened condensed milk over low heat just until pieces are melted and mixture is smooth. Remove from heat. Stir in lime peel and lime juice. Stir in nuts. Spread mixture evenly in prepared pan. Cover and chill about 2 hours or until set. Lift fudge from pan using edges of foil. Peel off foil; cut into pieces. Store in an airtight container at room temperature for up to 1 week or in the freezer for up to 2 months. Makes 2 1/2 pounds.

Mace Pound Cake

Contributed by Valerie Stone

Ingredients
½ cup Shortening
½ pound Butter
3 cups Sugar
1 cups Cake Flour
1 teaspoon Baking Powder
½ teaspoon Mace
1 teaspoon Vanilla
1 cup Milk
5 eggs

Instructions
Mix together the shortening, butter, sugar, and eggs. Sift together cake flour, baking powder, mace. Add vanilla to the milk. Alternate adding flour and milk mixtures, starting and ending with flour. Grease and flour a cake pan. Place in a cold oven at 350 degrees for 1 ½ hours. Let cool for 30 min. before removing from the pan.

"Seize the moment. Remember all those women on the Titanic who waved off the dessert cart."
~Erma Bombeck

Red, White and Mu Pie

Contributed by Lauren Goodwin

Ingredients
1 package of refrigerated pie crust
1 quart fresh strawberries
4 to 8 1 ounces squares white chocolate
1 8 ounces package of cream cheese
3/4 cup cold milk
1 package of white chocolate instant pudding
   or vanilla pudding
1.5 cups fresh blueberries
1 8 ounces container of Cool Whip

For a creamier pie, double the amount of cream cheese, milk and pudding for your pie

Instructions
Preheat oven to 425°F. Place the crust in a pie plate. Prick the bottom and sides of the crust with a fork. Bake for 10 to 12 minutes or until golden brown. Cool completely. Select about eight uniformly sized strawberries for dipping. Cut the selected strawberries in half through the stem ends. Thinly slice the remaining strawberries. Melt the white chocolate. Dip the strawberry halves in the melted chocolate. Place them on a sheet of parchment paper, with the cut side of the strawberry down.

124

Scrape the remaining melted chocolate over the bottom of the prepared pie crust, spreading evenly to coat the entire bottom and sides of crust. Refrigerate for 15 minutes or until the chocolate is set. Layer the sliced strawberries over the bottom of the crust. Beat the cream cheese. Gradually whisk in the milk until well blended. Slowly add the pudding mix, constantly stirring, and whisk until the mixture begins to thicken. Pour and smooth the mixture evenly over the strawberries. Spread the blueberries evenly over the entire top of pie filling. Decorate the top with a ring of Cool Whip and arrange the dipped strawberries on top at the outer edge of pie, stem side out. Place a small amount of cool whip in the center with one dipped whole strawberry. Refrigerate the pie to chill before serving.

ΦΜ

S'mores Nachos

Contributed by Vanessa Hall

Ingredients
1 box graham crackers
1 package marshmallows
Chocolate bars
Peanut butter cups (optional)

Instructions
Line the side of the bowl with graham crackers so they are resting against the sides with the bottom of the bowl clear. Place chocolate bar in bottom of bowl, then line the sides about halfway up the side of the bowl with chocolate bars. Cover bowl with marshmallows.

Heat in microwave in increments. The marshmallows will expand in the microwave. Before the marshmallows spill over the side, stop the microwave each time they expand and wait about 10-15 seconds then resume microwaving until the chocolate melts.

Variations:
Place peanut butter cups on bottom of bowl and line sides with chocolate.

Welsh Cakes

Contributed by Meghan Thomas

Ingredients
3 cups flour
1 cup sugar
1 teaspoon baking powder
1 teaspoon baking soda
½ to 1 teaspoon nutmeg *optional*
1 cup raisins
¾ cup Crisco
2 eggs
1 cup milk (may use more if needed to form a
  dough)
1 teaspoon vanilla

Instructions
Heat oven to 350 degrees. Combine flour, sugar, baking powder, baking soda, and nutmeg in a large bowl. Add Crisco, eggs, milk, and vanilla. Mix well. If needed, add extra milk to create a dough. Mix in raisins.

Form small sized balls out of the dough, and place apart on a cookie sheet. Bake for 10 to 15 minutes.

Microwave Peanut Brittle

Contributed by Meghan Cusack

Ingredients
1 cup sugar
½ cup light corn syrup
1 cup raw peanuts, or use unsalted dry
   roasted; almonds and walnuts are good too.
1/8 tsp salt
1 tsp vanilla
1 tsp baking soda

Instructions
Combine first 4 ingredients in 2-quart microwave safe, glass or stone-wear bowl. Microwave on HIGH for 8 minutes, stirring after 4 minutes (do not use a plastic spoon or a spoon that will transfer heat). Add vanilla. Microwave on HIGH for 2 minutes. Brittle should not get too brown. Stir in the baking soda until light and foamy. Spread on greased baking sheet as thinly as possible. Be very careful the candy is extremely hot. Allow to cool before breaking into pieces.

Uncle Tony's Revised Cocoa Peanut Butter Cookies

Contributed by Elaine Yang

Ingredients
1 stick butter
1¾ cup of sugar
¼ cup milk
4 tablespoons cocoa powder
1 tablespoon vanilla extract
½ cup creamy peanut butter
2 cups quick cooking oats

Instructions
Combine and bring butter, milk, sugar, cocoa powder, vanilla to a hard boil. Continue hard boil for 90 seconds. Remove from heat and stir in peanut butter and oats. When peanut butter has melted, drop big heaping tablespoons of mixture onto wax paper. Let cool and serve.

"Stressed spelled backwards is desserts. Coincidence? I think not!"
~Author Unknown

ဢ QUICK SUBSTITUTES ಐ

Sometimes, you are just missing *that one* little ingredient. In a pinch you can use these quick substitutions.

Baking Powder – Use 1/4 teaspoon baking soda and 5/8 teaspoon cream of tartar. OR use 1/4 teaspoon baking soda plus 1/2 cup buttermilk and reduce the liquid in the recipe by 1/2 cup.

Butter – Substitute 7/8 cup shortening to replace each 1 cup of butter. You can also use 7/8 cup of vegetable oil.

Buttermilk – Put 1 tablespoon of vinegar or lemon juice in a cup measure and add enough milk to make 1 cup. OR Substitute the same amount of plain yogurt.

Chocolate, Unsweetened – Use 3 tablespoons unsweetened cocoa powder plus 1 tablespoon butter for each ounce needed

Chocolate, Semi-sweet – Use 1 ounce of unsweetened chocolate plus 1 tablespoon sugar

Corn Starch - 3 tablespoons of all-purpose flour can be substituted.

Crumbs, Bread – Substitute 3/4 cups of cracker crumbs for 1 cup of bread crumbs.

Crumbs, Cracker – Substitute1 1/4 cups of bread crumbs for 1 cup of cracker crumbs.

Flour as a thickening agent – 1 tablespoon corn starch can be substituted.

Flour, Cake – Sift all-purpose flour and then remove 2 tablespoons from each cup.

Flour, Self-rising – Add 1 1/2 teaspoons baking powder and 1/8 teaspoon salt to each cup of flour.

Lemon Juice – An equal amount of vinegar can be substituted.

Sour Cream – Substitute 1 cup of plain yogurt OR 3/4 cup sour milk or buttermilk plus 1/3 cup of butter.

"The ability to quote is a serviceable substitute for wit."
~ W. Somerset Maugham

❧ MEASUREMENTS ❧

Liquid Measures

1 cup	8 fl oz	½ pint	237 mL	16 Tbsp
2 cups	16 fl oz	1 pint	473 mL	
4 cups	32 fl oz	1 quart	946 mL	
2 pints	32 fl oz	1 quart	0.946 L	
4 quarts	128 fl oz	1 gallon	3.785 L	
8 quarts	one peck			
4 pecks	one bushel			
Dash less than 1/4 tsp				
1 tsp	1/6 fl oz	5 gm	~5 mL	
1 Tbsp	½ fl oz	15 gm	15 mL	3 tsp
2 Tbsp	1 fl oz	30 gm	29.6 mL	1/8 cup
8 Tbsp	4 fl oz	¼ pint	118.5 mL	½ cup
fl oz – fluid ounce gm – gram L- liter mL – milliliter Tbsp – tablespoon tsp – teaspoon				

Dry Measures

3 tsp	1 Tbsp	1/2 oz	14.3 gm	
2 Tbsp	1/8 cup	1 oz	28.35 gm	
4 Tbsp	1/4 cup	2 oz	56.7 gm	
5 1/3 Tbsp	1/3 cup	2.6 oz	75.6 gm	
8 Tbsp	1/2 cup	4 oz	113.4 gm	1 stick butter
12 Tbsp	3/4 cup	6 oz	.375 lb	170 gm
32 Tbsp	2 cups	16 oz	1 lb	453.6 gm
64 Tbsp	4 cups	32 oz	2 lb	907 gm

gm – gram
lb - pound
oz – ounce
Tbsp – tablespoon
tsp – teaspoon

INDEX

Cucumber Raita, 61
Dorm Friendly Iced Coffee,
   16
Dorm Friendly Peanut
   Butter and Banana
   Protein Smoothie, 18
Fried Buttery Potatoes, 60
Hot Artichoke Dip, 48
Iced Tea, 16
Indian Chai, 14
Mixed Fruit Smoothie, 20

Morning Smoothie, 18
Potato Leek Soup, 30
Protein Energy Smoothie,
   19
Quinoa Salad, 40
Summer Asparagus and
   Tomato Salad, 39
Sweet Potato Soup, 28
Vic's Famous Chow-Chow,
   55
White Chili, 105

www.ingramcontent.com/pod-product-compliance
Lightning Source LLC
Chambersburg PA
CBHW071004040426
42443CB00007B/647